Dip your brush in **clean** water and "paint" a stroke on the Magic Paper. Begin working from the top down. The stroke will linger long enough for you to critique it and to go on to another stroke. Gradually (about 5 minutes) the strokes will fade. By the time you get to the bott

for prac
and ove
can get
paints or get your brushes dirty.

SUPPLIES

To master brush stroke painting techniques as illustrated in this workbook, your investment in supplies can be quite minimal: three brushes and a single color of paint. Add patience and enthusiasm, and you'll soon be well on your way toward mastering brush stroke painting!

BRUSHES

In decorative painting, excellent quality art brushes are your most important tools. To try to work with inferior quality or improperly cared for brushes is frustrating and unproductive. If necessary, skip the movies for a week, give up smoking, or skimp on groceries — whatever it takes to stash away a few extra coins to treat yourself to good brushes.

To begin, you can make do with three synthetic brushes — a flat, a round, and a liner. Later, you will want to add other sizes of these three types of brushes to your collection. The synthetic brushes can be used with all types of artists' paints, and are particularly well suited to acrylics. As you become more experienced, if you are working in oils or watercolors, you may wish to try the more expensive red sable; but, in the beginning, and for acrylics, good quality synthetics are your best investment.

The three brushes in Loew-Cornell's Jackie Shaw Basic Brush Kit have been specifically selected to help launch you into decorative painting with good quality brushes at affordable prices. Loew-Cornell's Jackie Shaw Decorative Folk Art Brush Kit contains seven additional brushes you will want as you gain experience. Ask for the kits at your favorite craft or art supply store. Or, write for ordering information to: Decorative Design Studio, Old Stone Mill, Route 3, Box 155, Smithsburg, MD 21783

See page 22 for care and handling of your brushes.

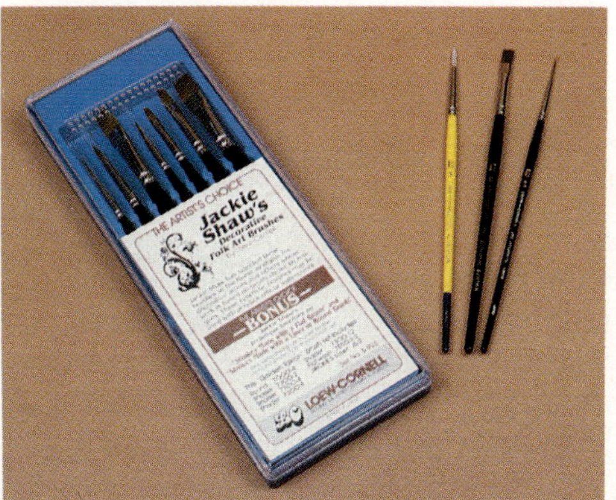

Loew-Cornell's Jackie Shaw brush kits.

PAINTS

Use whatever artists' paints you have. Or, if you have none, ask your craft or art store to recommend an acrylic paint for you. There are a number of very fine brands available. Acrylics are water soluble when wet, permanent when dry. Acrylics in jars are already liquified a bit, and thus readily lend themselves to strokework. For this reason, I recommend jar acrylics to my students. Tube acrylics will need to be thinned considerably with water. Likewise, oil paints will need to be thinned with thinner and a painting medium, which your craft or art store dealer can help you select.

MISCELLANEOUS

Styrofoam meat trays or plates. These make satisfactory palettes (surfaces on which to squeeze out paints to be loaded into brushes). When you decide you're hooked on painting, buy one less half gallon of ice cream for the family or yourself, and indulge in a disposable paper palette — a pad of fifty sheets of treated paper which may be torn off and discarded after a painting session. Be sure to get a palette designed for use with the type of paint you're using.

Jar. This will hold water (for acrylics) or thinner (for oils) for rinsing brushes and thinning paints. HINT: Pass up the next movie you plan to see (wait for the home video) and instead, treat yourself to a brush basin — a compartmentalized container for soaking and washing brushes.

An old butter knife or plastic knife. This will serve as a palette knife for inter-mixing and thinning paints until next week when you forego four sodas or one small cocktail and pocket your savings for a trip to the craft store.

Paper towels. No expense there, just sneak them from the kitchen. Old, soft cloths (rags) will also do.

Scrap paper, newsprint, used computer paper, grocery bags (not the plastic ones) — for practicing work.

Tracing paper, clear acetate, or a piece of glass with edges taped for safety — for practicing. See page 8 and the back cover.

GET A FEEL FOR YOUR BRUSHES

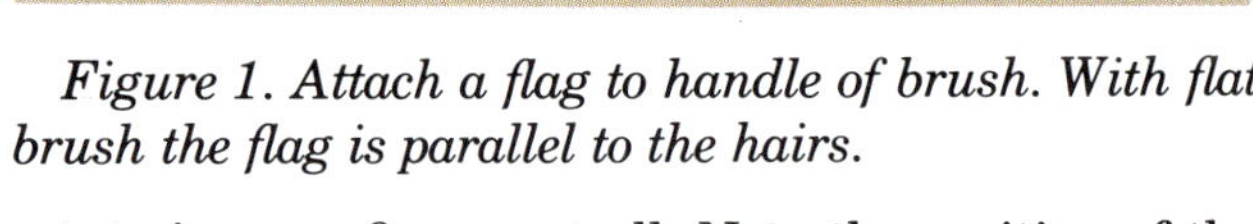

Figure 1. Attach a flag to handle of brush. With flat brush the flag is parallel to the hairs.

TWO CATEGORIES OF BRUSH STROKES:

There are two categories of brush strokes:

1. Those made with a flat brush, and —

2. Those made with a liner or a round brush.

For recording your progress in the book, practice first with the flat brush, then the liner. After you have mastered the liner, you should be able easily to do all those same strokes with the round brush. The round brush strokes will generally be a little shorter and fuller; the liner strokes, more flowing and graceful.

FLAG YOUR BRUSHES

In many cases the movement of the brush in forming a stroke is described in terms of hands on a clock. (See "S" stroke, Page 11.) To take advantage of these descriptions, you should attach a masking tape or paper flag to the tip of the brush handle as shown in Figure 1. The flag and hairs of the **flat** brush should be parallel. The flag may point any way on the **round** and **liner**. Carefully read the directions for forming each brush stroke, noting any reference to the position of the flag. If no mention is made regarding a change in position of the flag from start to finish, then the brush must not rotate in your fingers at all. Note the position of the flag at the beginning of the stroke. Then be sure it stays in that position throughout the stroke.

Many strokes are formed through pressure and release of pressure rather than through rotation of the brush.

Those which do involve brush rotation in your fingers are carefully described.

LOADING THE BRUSH

There are several ways of loading paint into the brush. Three of the most common, used for strokework, are described below. Of these, the easiest is the full load; and this is the one with which you should begin your studies. Later, when you can execute the strokes easily you might wish to begin experimenting with the side load and double load (primarily for flat brushes only). While the emphasis of this book is on brush **strokes** rather than brush **loading**, a brief description of the loading techniques is included below to help you further develop your skill once you've mastered the strokes.

FULL LOADING

With a little moisture in the brush, dip half the length of the hairs into the edge of a puddle of paint. Stroke the brush on the palette to work paint well up towards the metal ferrule. Stroke over and over in the same spot continually adding more paint. This action will help move the paint up **into** the brush, rather than leaving globs of paint clinging to the outside edges of the brush. Working over and over **in the same spot** rather than stroking in different spots all over the palette, will feed the brush instead of exhausting its supply of paint. If the paint feels too stiff to move easily, add a little more moisture (water or thinner) to it. (See Figure 2.)

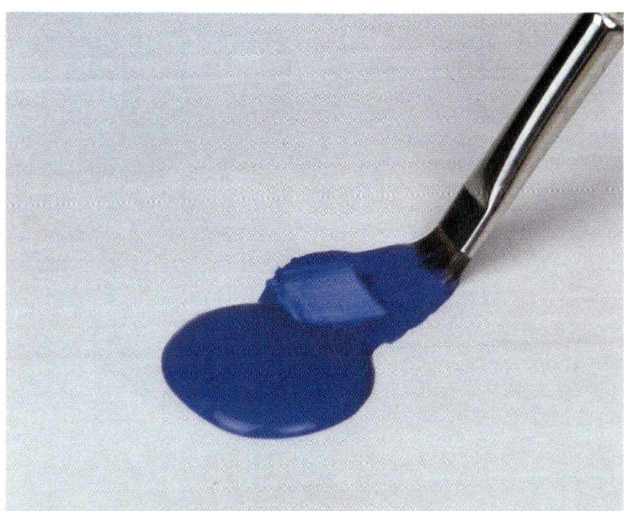

Figure 2. Full loading.

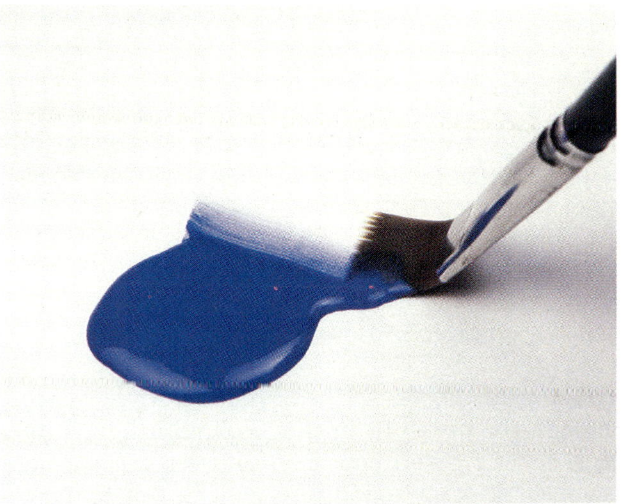

Figure 3. Side loading, picking up initial load of paint.

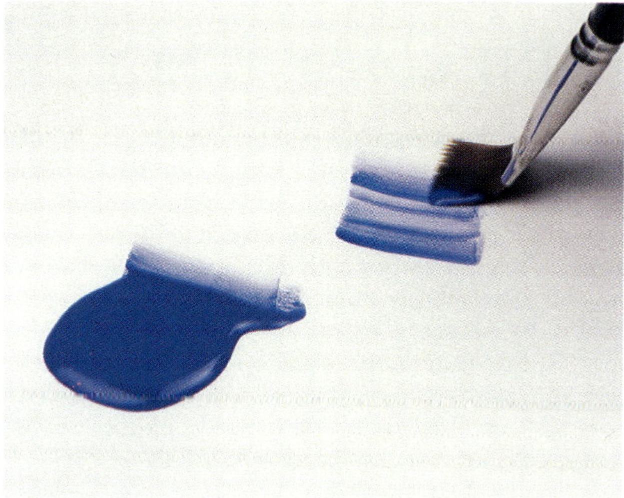

Figure 4. Side loading, "walking" the brush sideways to spread paint.

SIDE LOADING

Paint, either thick from the jar, or thinned with water to create a transparent wash, is picked up on the edge of a slightly damp brush by sliding the brush hairs alongside the puddle of paint (Figure 3). Paint is then worked gradually across the hairs to create a gradated tone ranging from intense color to a scant hint of color. This is done by stroking the brush, over and over in the same spot (no longer than 1 inch), and "walking" slightly to the right then to the left, back and forth until gradual blending is accomplished. (See Figure 4.)

Note: Until you become quite masterful in "walking" back and forth and gobbling the paint up into the hairs by applying proper pressure, "walk" only one-half the width of the brush. This will eliminate the possibility of your getting paint on the non-paint edge of the brush when you begin to "walk" back to your starting position.

It will be necessary to load more paint into the brush as it is worked both up into the hairs toward the ferrule and across the hairs toward the damp edge. Once thoroughly loaded, the brush may be quickly and easily replenished while painting with more paint or a scant bit of water. The initial loading of a color needs to be carefully done, and may take you a while to master. A drop of water on the palette is handy for restoring proper dampness to the brush. Dip the non-paint side of the brush in the water drop, then touch it briefly to a damp paper towel to remove excess water. Otherwise puddles will occur in your stroking.

DOUBLE LOADING

Follow the procedure for side loading, but this time pick up a different color on each half of the brush. Stroke the double-loaded brush on the palette as for side loading, walking left and right, until the two colors merge in the center creating a third color. For instance, if you load blue on one side, yellow on the other, after stroking and blending on the palette, you should have green in the center. (The blue and yellow should still be obvious on their respective sides.) Reload to fill the brush thoroughly, being sure, however, that no blobs cling to the brush. Paint should be worked well **into** the hairs for double loading and side loading. (See Figure 5.)

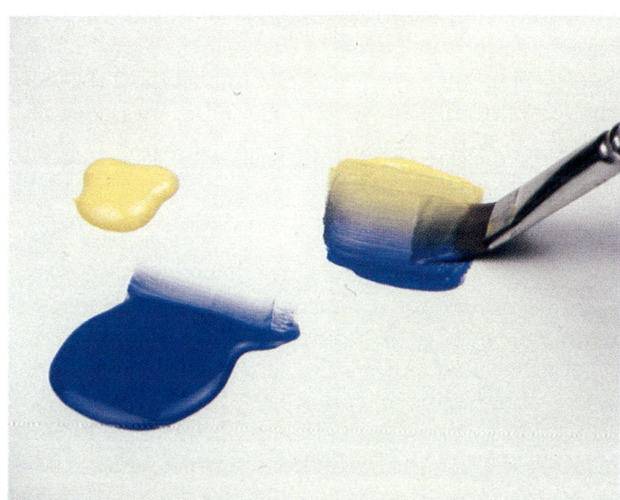

Figure 5. Double loading.

Remember, load the brush thoroughly. A couple of quick dabs in the paint puddle is not thorough. Apply pressure in loading paint into the brush by stroking firmly through the edge of the paint, permitting the brush to grab the paint and hold as much in its hairs as possible without globs clinging to the edges. So many difficulties in mastering brush control can be eliminated with proper loading techniques.

PAINT CONSISTENCY

Different brush strokes and techniques call for different paint consistencies. For long, continuous strokes, the paint must be thinned considerably so that it can flow through the brush. To create textured brush strokes, one must work with thicker paint. The following four consistencies, described in terms of recognizable dairy products, should help you determine how much to thin your paints to achieve the effect you seek.

1. 1% or non-fat milk — an almost ink-like consistency; good for long scrolls, spirals, coils.

2. Light cream — less runny than above; good for both flat and round (or liner) strokes, especially when a number are to be repeated as in a border design.

3. Heavy cream — this will give you more fully bodied strokes, but the brush will have to be reloaded more often than with the light cream mixture.

4. Sour cream — rich, heavy texture here; nice for short stokes where lots of dimension is desired. Particularly effective with round brush and liner.

As a general rule, in the beginning, while working through the exercises in this book, use the 1% milk consistency for warm up liner exercises, and the light cream for all other, round, liner, and flat brush strokes.

MASTERING BRUSH CONTROL

Read the hints below once a day before you begin painting. Think of them while you paint. And, review them again and again and again — until their execution becomes a part of your usual handling of the brush. Then.... you will master brush control.

1. **Paint from your shoulder — not with your fingers.** As a brushstroke artist, particularly a freehanding one, you have two vitally important tools: your brush and, of all things, your shoulder. To try to use your brush without also using your shoulder is about as futile as trying to use a sewing machine without electricity. The machine **can** be cranked by hand, but what a jerky, awkward, and tiring way to sew. How much smoother, surer, and more flowing the stitchery would be if only you'd plug in the machine and take advantage of the power source. The same thing is true in painting. You can crank out the brush strokes by hand — a laborious and often jerky process; or you can engage the "power source" and let the strokes flow smoothly and rhythmically from your shoulder. Until you've mastered the freedom of working with your shoulder and entire arm (rather than with only brush and fingers) you cannot appreciate what a vast difference this can make in your stroke painting. **Of all the hints I will be sharing with you throughout this book, this one, without a doubt, will make the greatest difference in helping you master brush control and develop your own freehanding skill and spontaneous style.**

2. **Let your arm hang freely.** Sit comfortably. Ideally, you should work at a low table, or on a high stool or, preferably, in your lap so that your entire arm is free to move. If you are having to hitch your shoulder up in order to paint on a table, you are not comfortable (as you'll soon discover via a pain across your back, neck, or shoulder).

3. **Use your little finger for support, leverage, pivoting.** With your arm hanging freely from your shoulder, keep your wrist, forearm, and elbow off the table! No resting on anything except your little finger-and that **should never be stationary**. It must move freely as an extension of your arm, all moving as a single unit. The little finger may be extended or curved under, whichever way you find most comfortable (both ways will seem awkward initially, so just keep working on it). The little finger serves as a pivot, a support for your arm, and a lever helping you to control thick/thin pressure and release on strokes. Use it to advantage.

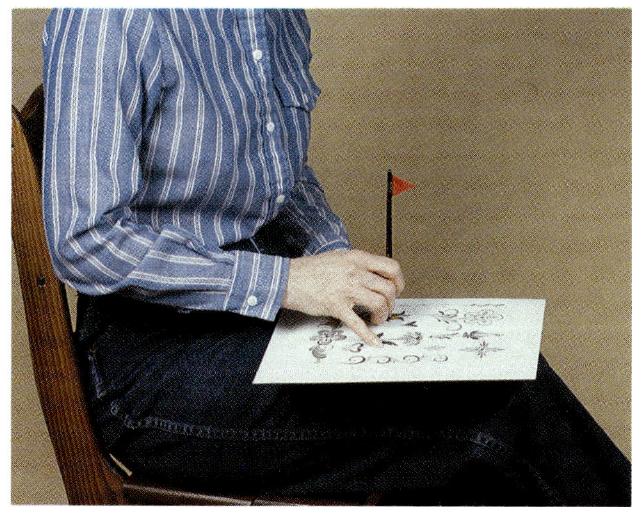

Figure 1. Painting in lap, balancing on little finger, with brush perpendicular to surface.

4. **Hold the brush perpendicular to your painting surface.** This gives you the greatest control, easily permitting you to apply and release pressure for thick/thin strokes, and to allow brush hairs to begin on knife edge, or point, and return to same at the completion of the stroke. Avoid holding the brush as you would a pen or pencil — laid back and relaxed in your hand.

5. **Stay in control of the brush at all times.**

a. **Slow down, stop, lift off.** Near the ends of strokes, slow down to permit hairs to return to natural formation (chisel edge for flat, point for round or liner). Come to a complete stop. Then lift off. Rarely is a stroke to be completed in mid air — that is, lifting off before letting hairs return to chisel or point, and before a complete stop.

b. **Let the handle pull the hairs of the brush.** None of the beginning strokes in this book call for pushing the hairs. The rare strokes which are executed with a push rather than a pull are discussed in *Jackies Freehanding Seminar, Book 1.* Experiment with pushing and pulling the hairs to see why this procedure is so important. When you **pull** the hairs of the brush, they follow the handle, and you're in control of where they will go. (See Figure 2.) When you **push** the hairs with the handle, you have no control. The hairs separate and go where they please. (See Figure 3.)

c. **Lean into the curves.** Let your brush handle lean slightly around curved strokes just as you would on a bicycle going round a curve on the road. This leaning helps permit the hairs to **follow** the handle. (See Figure 4.)

6. **Strive for contrast through pressure and release.** Develop a flowing rhythm of pressure and release, always thinking contrast, **contrast!** Create exciting artistic and visual impact with variations in thick and thin, long and short, nearly straight and very curvy. Be expressive. Give your brush work some punch, some flair, some style that says, "I did it; I'm glad I did it; and I loved doing it"!!

7. **Paint confidently and with authority.** Put strokes down and leave them alone. Whatever may happen at the end of your brush, reject the temptation to try to paint over it, to improve it. To do so almost always results in a situation worse than the original, less-than-perfect stroke. Leave it alone, and though others may not understand it, at least they will assume you meant it since you left it there.

8. **Practice!** Great pianists practice daily, great skaters skate daily, great runners run daily, great painters paint daily. Get the picture? Be patient with yourself and remember that (according to poet Piet Hein) TTT — "Things take time."

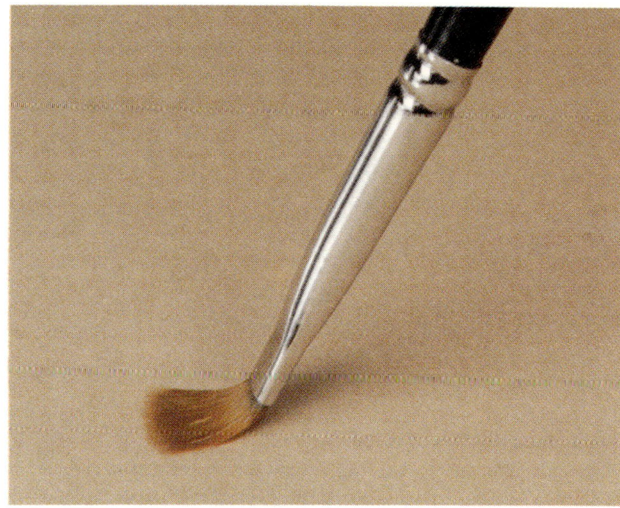

Figure 2. Handle pulling brush — right!

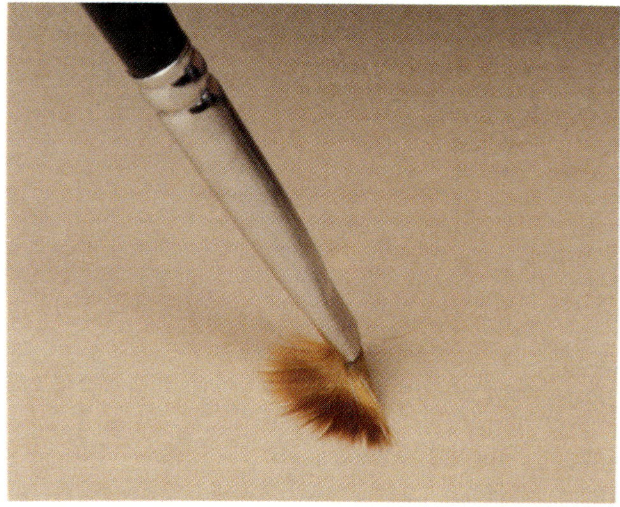

Figure 3. Handle pushing brush — wrong! Hairs are bent so sharply that control is lost.

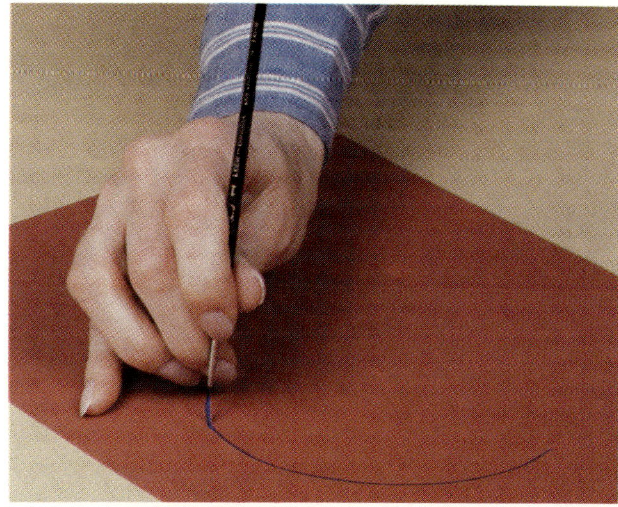

Figure 4. Brush leans into curve, just like a bicycle.

PRACTICE PAGE

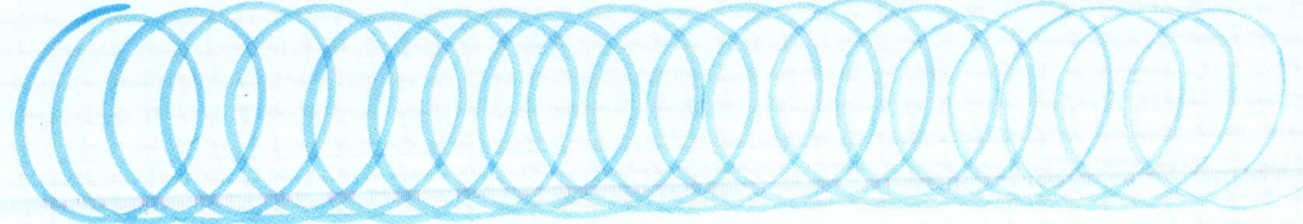

Strive for regularity, uniformity. Practice the stroke in all directions.

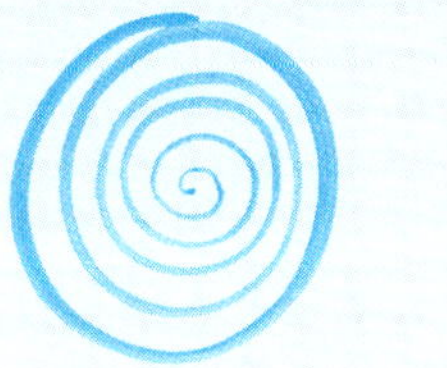

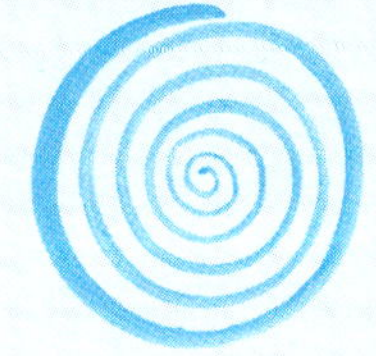

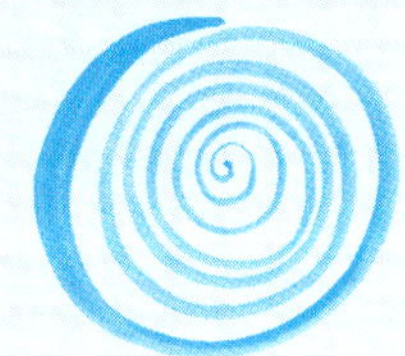

Lay tracing paper on this page (or clear acetate or a sheet of glass with edges taped for safety). With paint in your brush, practice any of the strokes with which you're having difficulty. Do not worry about matching the shape and size exactly of the strokes on this page. Just use them as a guide.

If you get angles here instead of graceful curves, review page 15.

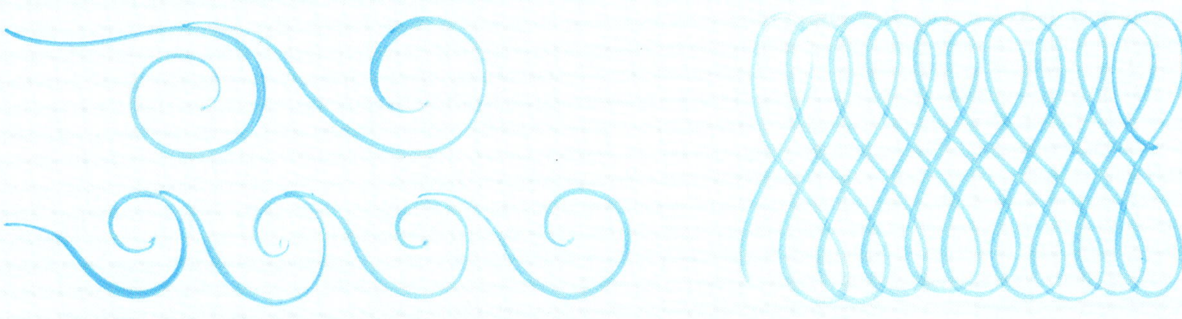

Is your paint thin enough, or are you getting skipped places? How is your contrast? Exciting? Non-existent?

Remember: Slow down, let the hairs return to their natural shape, stop, *then* lift off.

Keep that brush perpendicular to painting surface.

Did you lean into the curve? Are you remembering to balance on your little finger?

Did the handle of the brush *always* pull the hairs?

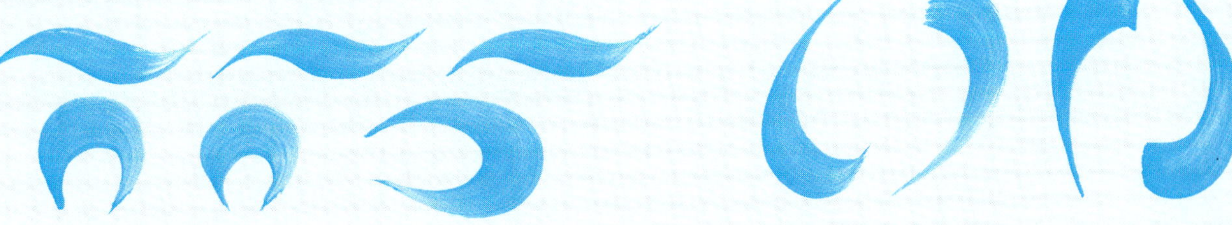

Keep the flag pointing to the outside edge of the crescent to avoid flips. Are you painting from your shoulder?

Jackie Shaw's
DECORATIVE DESIGN STUDIO

FREEHAND BRUSHSTROKE PRACTICE SHEET

USE THIS PAGE FOR PRACTICE OR NOTES

BROAD AND CHISEL STROKES

FLAT BRUSH

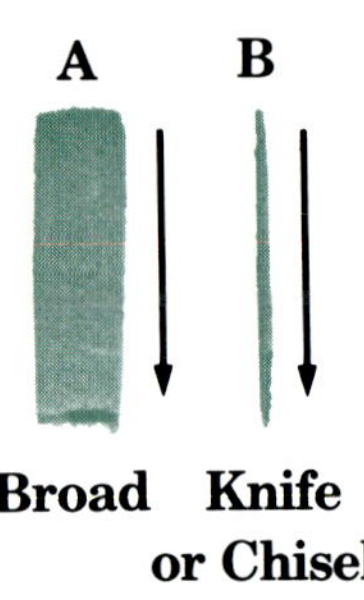

A. This is the broad side of the brush. Used in this position, it will paint a stroke the width of the brush, or even wider if pressure is applied. Begin and end with the brush held perpendicular to painting surface. This will give clean, crisp edges.

B. The chisel stroke is done on the "knife edge" of the brush and results in a narrow, straight line. Apply **no** pressure; rather, hold the brush perpendicular and pull towards you with even pressure.

Work with these two strokes until you have good control over each. In combinations, they will be the basis of all the other flat brush strokes you learn in this book. Once you've mastered them, pulling the strokes toward you, try pulling to the left and the right and away from you. Some directions will be easier for you than others.

Now you try it. Thin paint very slightly with water. Record your progress. Jot down today's date.

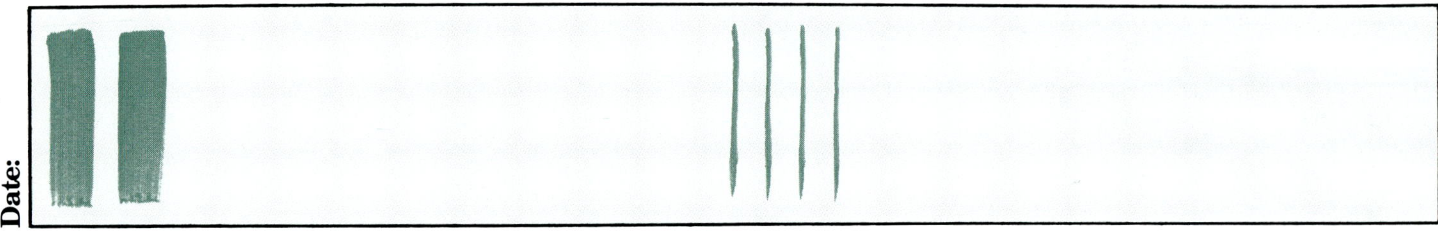

Make a real effort to keep your brush handle perpendicular to the painting surface. Strive for crisp, even lines and edges. Extra effort in developing control now will pay off later.

WHOOPS! Study your first painted samples above. Look for any trouble spots as illustrated below. Mark the troublesome areas with a pen as a reminder where to direct your attention.

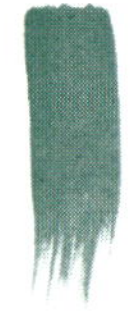

Hey, where's your self control? You had a nice beginning but in your eagerness to get through, you forgot to slow down, stop, let hairs return to a chisel edge, then lift off.

Two factors could cause ragged edges. 1) Brush is not held perpendicular — laying too flat to painting surface. 2) Brush is in bad condition causing hairs to separate.

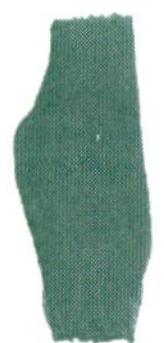

Bulges are caused by uneven pressure.

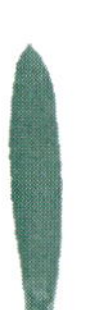

Pressure is too heavy. Skim along painting surface.

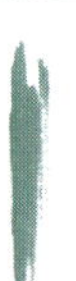

Brush is not in good condition. Dried paint has been allowed to remain near ferrule causing the brush hairs to bulge.

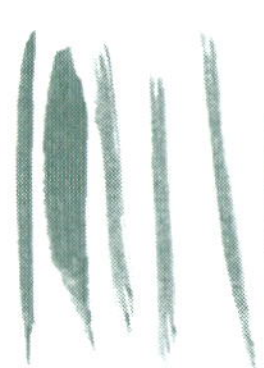

Haphazard practicing. Slow down. Be precise.

Now then, with all your trouble spots noted, turn to the Magic Paper on page 9 and practice with water. Later today, tomorrow, or next week when you feel you have greatly improved, return to this page and paint a follow-up sample. Be sure to date it and record your progress.

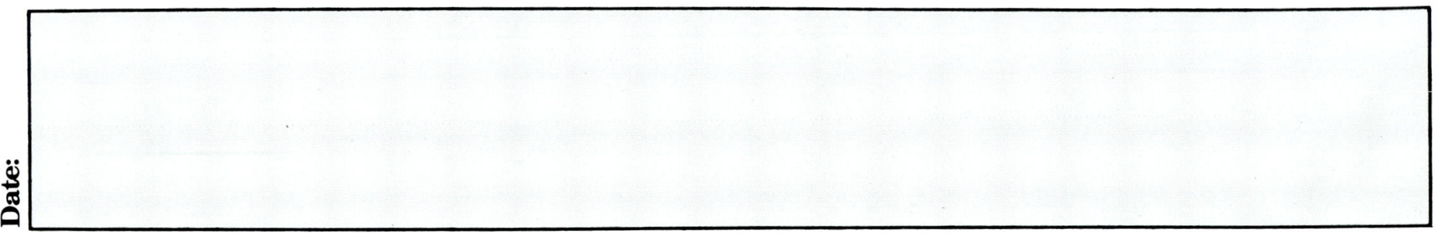

Are you having fun yet? Just think: the mastery of these rather plain strokes, and those in the pages to follow, will open up a whole new world to you.

"S" STROKE

FLAT BRUSH

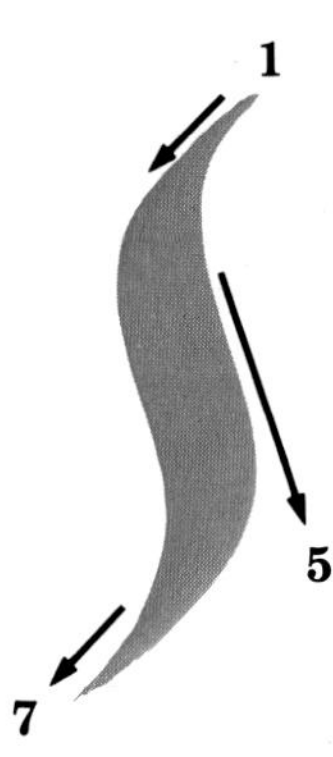

This stroke is commonly called the "S" stroke, though it is not as sharply curved as an "S." Its curve is gentle, flowing, like the Hogarth curves named for William Hogarth who determined the most graceful line in art. (Look him up in your library and see the lines he experimented with.) This stroke uses both strokes practiced on the previous page - the knife or chisel and the broad. To begin, hold the brush with the flag pointing at 1 o'clock, slide on the chisel edge (toward 7 o'clock); gradually apply pressure and pull briefly toward 5 o'clock; release pressure gradually and continue sliding toward 7 o'clock. Flag should never move. It begins, continues, and ends pointing at 1 o'clock. The stroke is made by pulling, pressing and releasing. To paint an "S" facing the other direction, the flag points to 11 o'clock; brush slides on the chisel edge toward 5 o'clock; pressure is applied in pulling toward 7 o'clock, pressure is released and brush continues toward 5 o'clock. Go through the motions with your brush as you read the directions. When you think you understand, load the brush with paint and record your **first** strokes below. Don't wait until you've perfected the stroke to record it. That will serve no purpose. Remember to write in the date.

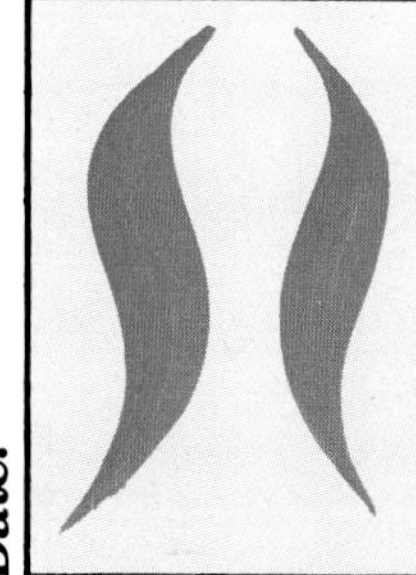

Date:

Did you find one direction to be much easier than the other? Good. You're normal. Keep practicing. Soon both ways will be comfortable. Then, you can try painting the "S's" upside down and sideways. Ultimately you will be able to paint strokes in **any** direction. Just remember, on this stroke, **the flag never rotates from its starting position.**

WHOOPS!

Too much pressure at the beginning of the stroke. Remember to **slide** first, then press.	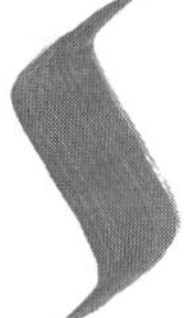 Directional changes too abrupt. Begin applying pressure a bit before changing directions, and release pressure a little before reversing direction back toward 7 o'clock.	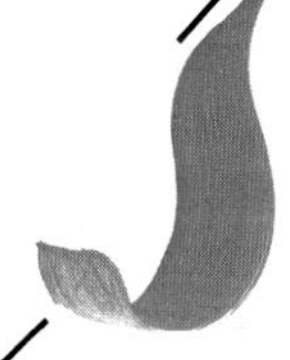 Too curvy. What happened to the flag? Remember, **flag position never changes**. The beginning and ending angles should be the same.
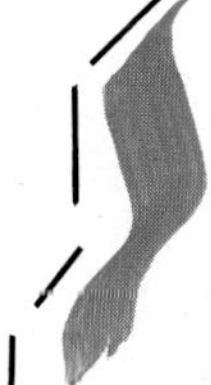 Confused about **when** to stop? The "S" stroke should have only three directional segments. The stroke above has four.	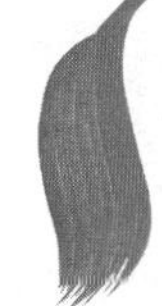 Fuzzy tails happen when you hurry. You're out of control. Review paragraph 5a on page 7 regarding how to stay in control of the brush.	This one's out of balance. Lower half is much longer than upper half.

Practice time! Turn to page 9. Be sure to rinse every bit of paint from your brush and use only water on the Magic Paper. This is often a difficult stroke for new painters to master. Be patient. You **will** get it.

Date:

If you continue to have difficulty with this stroke, draw lines as shown here and practice **on** the lines. That will give you the directional changes. Then all you have to worry about is the application and release of pressure.

SCROLL AND FLAT COMMAS

FLAT BRUSH

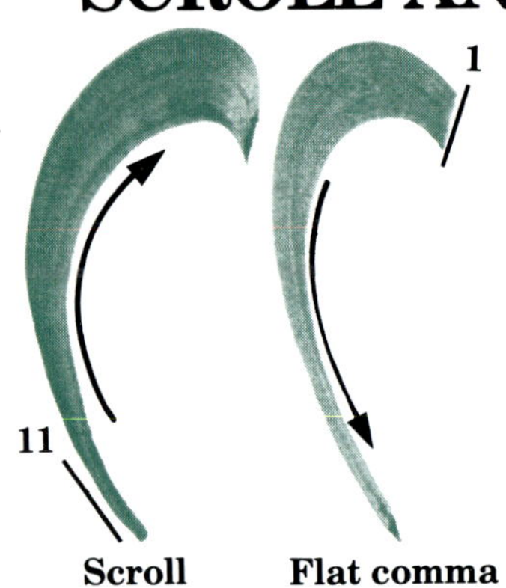

These two strokes look very similar but are made quite differently. Both use the chisel and broad strokes.

The **scroll** stroke (usually the more difficult of the two for beginners) begins with a chisel stroke and curves, flattening out into a broadstroke. It begins with the flag pointing to 11 o'clock. Try not to move the flag at all when making the stroke. To paint a stroke in the other direction, hold the flag at 1 o'clock.

The **flat comma,** on the other hand, begins with a broad stroke, curves slightly, and with gradual release of pressure, slides into a chisel stroke. Begin with the flag at 1 o'clock. A **very slight** rotation - no more than from 1 back to 11 o'clock - may be helpful.

You will likely find you prefer one of these strokes over the other. Never mind. Learn them both! Then also practice them in other directions - facing the opposite way as well as upside down. When you get expressive and fancy later, you will find that the scroll stroke lends itself to freer designing; the flat comma, to a bit more controlled effort. Practice here first, to give yourself a basis from which to review your growth. Write in the date.

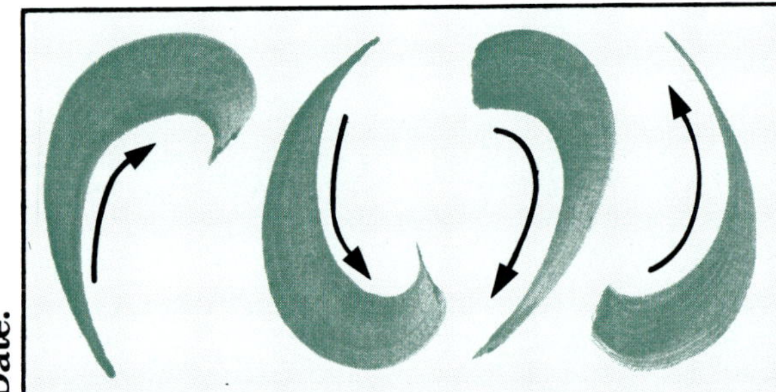

Date:

WHOOPS! Did you encounter any of these common problems? Mark the mistakes on your work above. Learn to critique your work positively. You'll improve **because** of your mistakes.

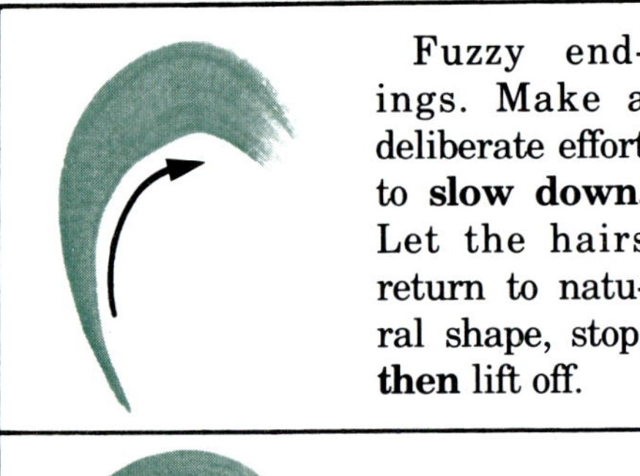

Fuzzy endings. Make a deliberate effort to **slow down.** Let the hairs return to natural shape, stop, **then** lift off.

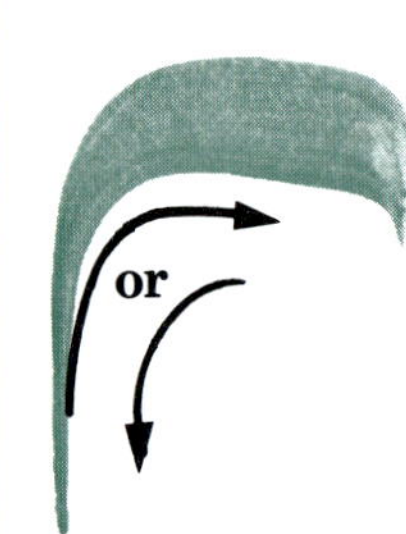

Too angular. Try not to head straight for 12 or 6 o'clock. Work for a more gentle curve and a less straight side.

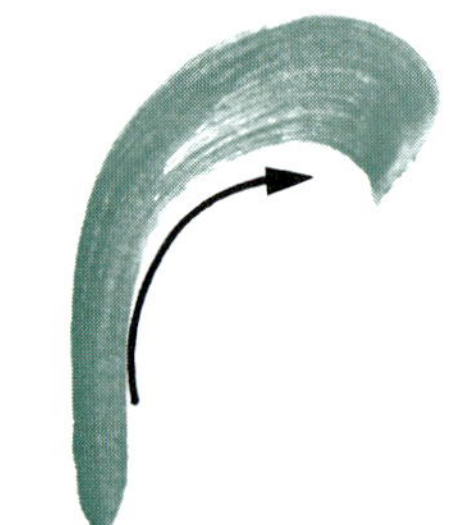

Too much pressure on chisel stroke. Slide more gently.

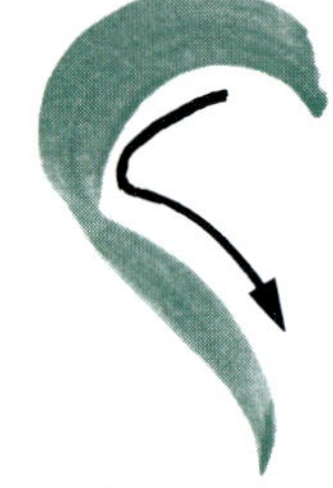

You've really **flipped** over this stroke. The stroke began with the handle leaning slightly to the left, then ended leaning slightly to the right. Try to keep handle at same tilt throughout stroke.

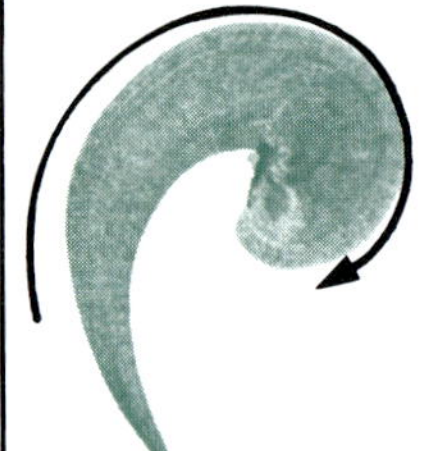

You're working too hard here and rotating the brush at the end. Remember, flag should not move.

Now with all that knowledge — of the things that can go awry — head for the Magic Paper on page 9 and work out the kinks. When you can see and feel progress, return to this page to record your successes.

Date:

How are you doing? Pretty good, eh? Don't you just love brushstrokes?

CRESCENT STROKE

FLAT BRUSH

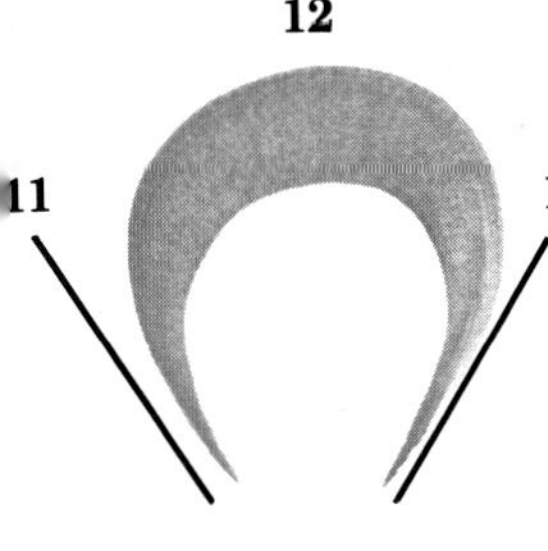

Like the previous strokes, this one also uses both the chisel and broad strokes. There are a number of variations on the stroke (as illustrated in **Jackie's Freehanding Seminar, Book 1**); however, this is the most common.

Begin with the flag pointing towards 11 o'clock. (Lefties, point your flag towards 1 o'clock.) Slide briefly on the chisel edge. Then apply pressure rounding the curve. The brush may rotate **very slightly.** Gradually release pressure, returning to the chisel and slide briefly. The flag should be at 1 o'clock (lefties, at 11 o'clock). Keep the brush perpendicular to painting surface. Think "round" as you paint to give the stroke a rounded, rather than squared, shape. Four or more of these painted around a center dot make a nice flower.

Now you try it. (Lefties, begin on the right and paint from right to left — 1 o'clock to 11 o'clock. This will enable you to see what you're painting as you paint.) Remember to write in the date.

Date:

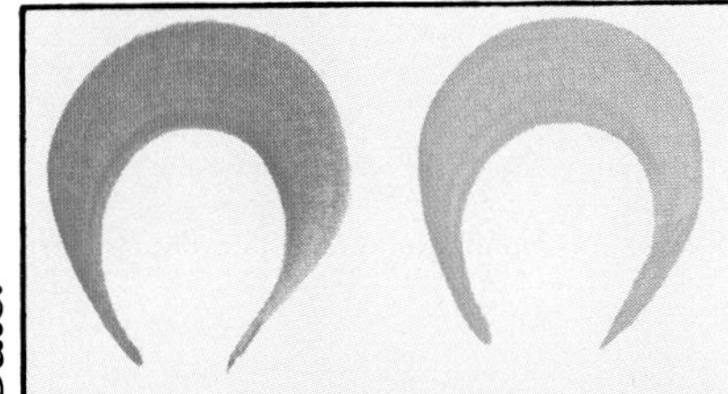

Lefties, start here

Are you remembering to balance on your little finger and to keep you wrist and arm off the table? Don't worry if your strokes aren't perfect yet. It's hard to **do**, and **remember**, so many things at once. Given time and practice, things will improve.

WHOOPS! Now let's look for common trouble spots.

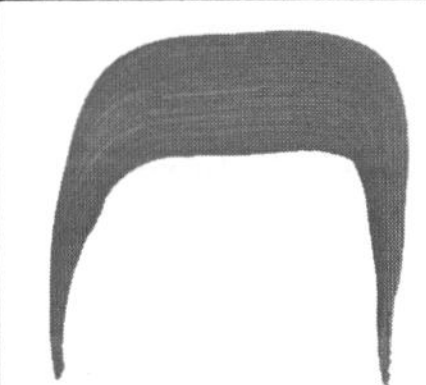 Edges are too square. You must think "round" to get rid of the corners. Change in pressure from chisel to broad to chisel is too abrupt. Gradually apply and release the pressure.	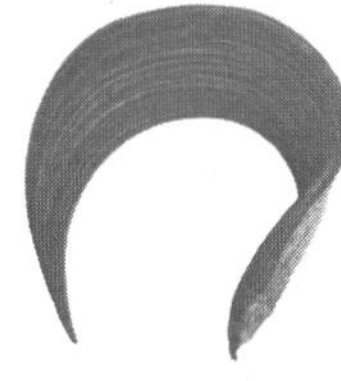 Did you flip over this stroke? As you begin the stroke, notice which hairs are going up across the top edge. These same hairs must keep to the outside edge as you complete the stroke. Remember to let the brush (flag) rotate slightly.
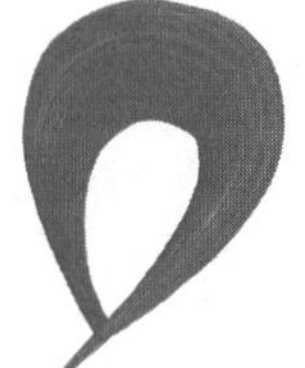 This stroke is closed in from too much hurry or too little control. Let there be an opening at the base; and be sure both right and left sides are the same length.	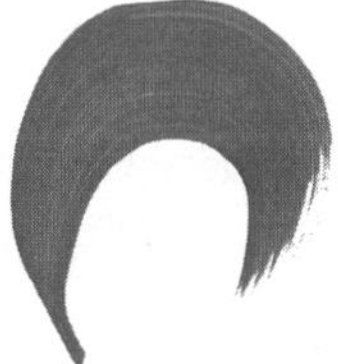 Ragged ending. Things done in a hurry are rarely done well. Tsk, tsk. **Slow down.**

O.K. Once you've located and noted your trouble spots, rinse your brush and begin working out on the Magic Paper. Practice the strokes from both left and right, sideways, and upside down. Find your best direction, but also work to perfect other directions.

Return to this page when you see improvement and record your progress.

Date:

Remember to practice your earlier strokes as you add new ones to your repertoire. Give yourself a pat on the back for me and keep up the good effort!

WARM UP LINER EXERCISE: SPIRAL

LINER AND ROUND BRUSH

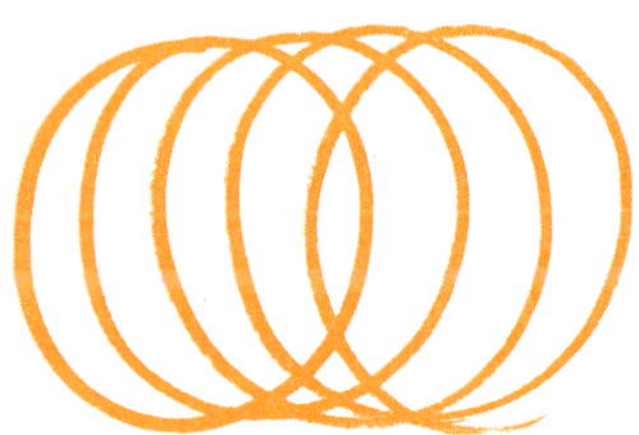

If you're old enough to remember the Palmer Method of handwriting, this exercise may look familiar. It is a good one to help you develop flowing motion, and steady, even control of the liner brush. **Think round and paint round.** Develop a rhythm as you paint the spirals, trying to space each loop evenly. Hold the brush perpendicular to the painting surface. Work from the tip of the brush and be sure that the loops are formed by the motion of your whole arm from your shoulder, not by your fingers. Imagine that your thumb and forefingers are immobile. Balance on your little finger, being sure that it **moves** with the rest of your arm. And remember, the brush hairs should always **follow** the handle.

Thin your paint to an almost ink-like consistency. Thoroughly load the brush and try to paint as long a spiral as possible with one loading.

Begin **Lefties, start here.**

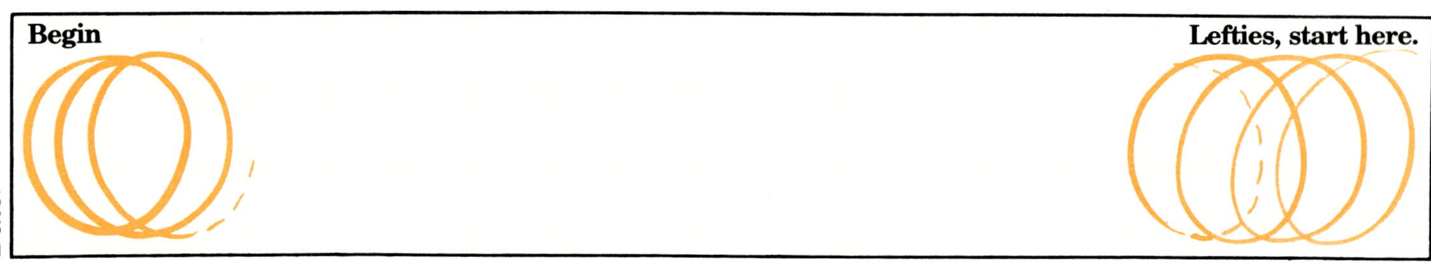

Date:

Strive for uniformity of thickness, rhythm, and size (about the size of a quarter).

WHOOPS! Well, how did you do? Study your first effort above. Compare it to the problem samples below. Review the directions at the top of the page and learn to critique your own work.

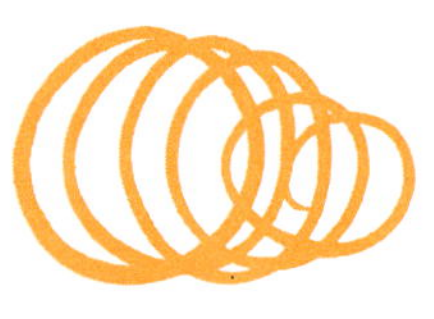

Inflation is so bad you've forgotten how big a quarter is. Don't be so uptight. Stretch the loops a little larger.

Little angular glitches like these may appear anywhere in the loop, and are caused by either: 1) moving thumb and fingers to **push** brush around rather than working from shoulder; 2) hesitating at the top and thinking "whew, I got to the top, now I go back down," thus; 3) forgetting to think **around** or over the top, and then down.

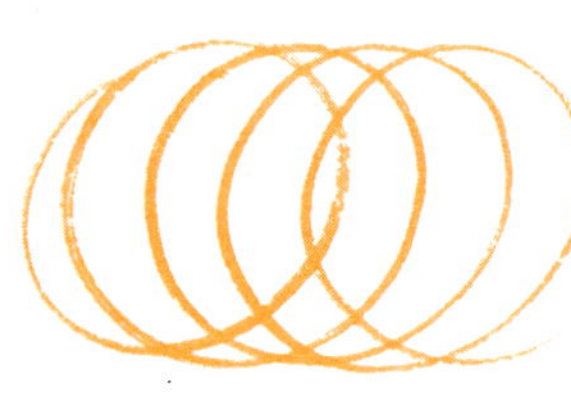

Paint is too dry or brush is insufficiently loaded. Paint should be quite thin, so it can feed through the brush hairs like ink in a pen reservoir. The brush should be thoroughly loaded until it can hold no more paint. Painting too fast can also cause skipped places.

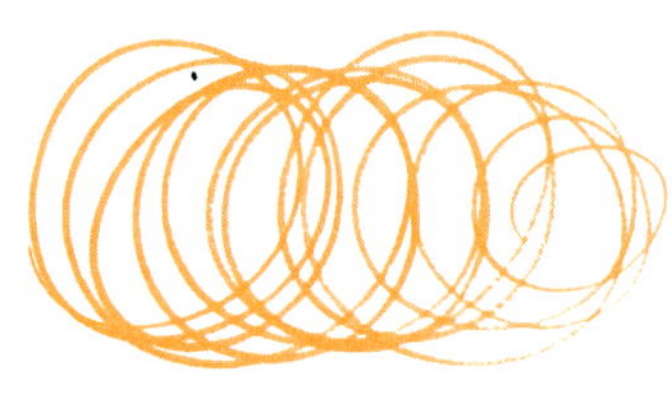

Where's the fire? Slow down. Be precise, rhythmic, uniform. You can become expressive and unique after you've mastered the techniques.

If you've isolated your weak areas, then turn to the MAGIC PAPER on page 9, and work out the kinks. Come back when you've improved and record your progress here.

Date:

Are you sitting comfortably? Or is your shoulder hunched up high — a sure sign of a pending pain in the neck. Review paragraph 2, page 6.

WARM UP EXERCISE: COIL

LINER AND ROUND BRUSH

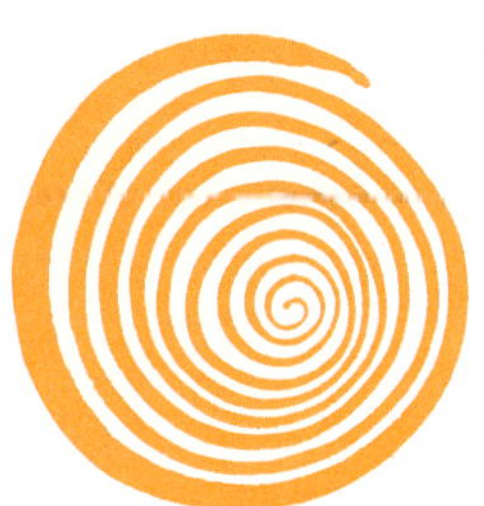

This exercise will help you develop pressure control — thick to thin, as well as skill in executing strokes which curve. To begin, hold the brush perpendicular to the painting surface and apply pressure to flatten approximately three-fourths of the length of the hairs. This will give the coil stroke a broad beginning around the outside edge. Spiral inward, gradually releasing pressure to create an increasingly thinner line. As you proceed around the curve, lean the handle of the brush into the curve, just as you would lean your body into a curve while riding a bicycle. This leaning will allow the hairs to follow the handle of the brush.

Now, you try it. Use paint thinned to a light cream consistency. Record your progress; jot down today's date.

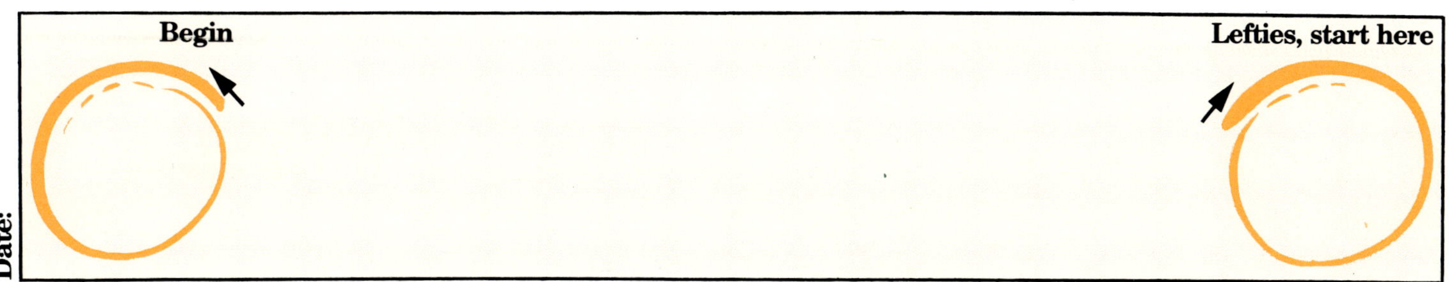

Paint slowly and deliberately. Try to paint the coils the same size as shown. Do not fret if yours are not perfect. They shouldn't be.......yet. **Give yourself time to learn, and more importantly, permission to be a learner.**

WHOOPS! Study your first painted samples above. Look for any trouble spots as illustrated below. Mark the troublesome areas with a pen as a reminder where to direct your attention.

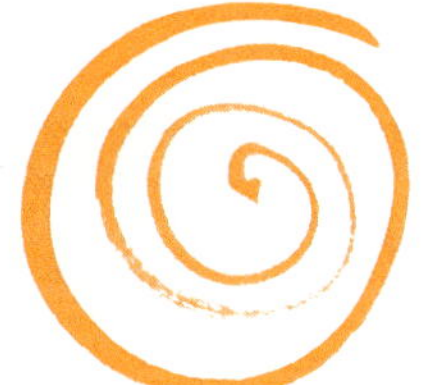

Whoa! Here's what happens when you work too fast. Slow down! Try to pack more coils in. Remember, be deliberate. Strive for even spacing between the coils.

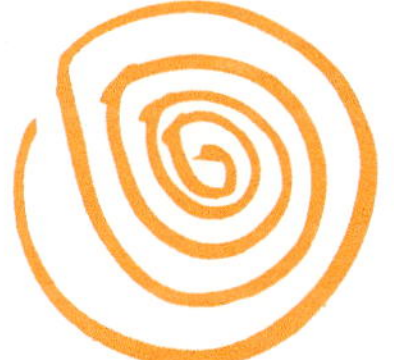

Little angular glitches may be caused by: 1) moving thumb and index finger instead of using shoulder; 2) trying to push the brush rather than letting the hairs follow the handle; 3) hesitating; 4) not thinking "around" the curve.

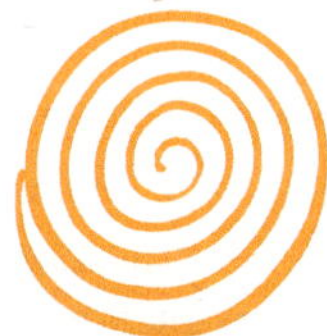

This looks nice and controlled. So what's wrong? Where is the thick and thin pressure variation? Press hard in the beginning so you will develop the skill of releasing pressure as you paint. You'll need that press/release skill later in other strokes.

O.K. Wash your brush and practice these in water on the MAGIC PAPER on page 9. When you think you've improved quite a bit — today, tomorrow, or next month — return to this page and paint a follow-up sample below. Be sure to date it.

Date:

Critique your work. Look for strengths as well as weaknesses. Smile at your progress, then forge ahead to another lesson. But keep practicing all strokes as you work through the book.

WARM UP EXERCISE: DOUBLE LOOPS OR FIGURE 8'S

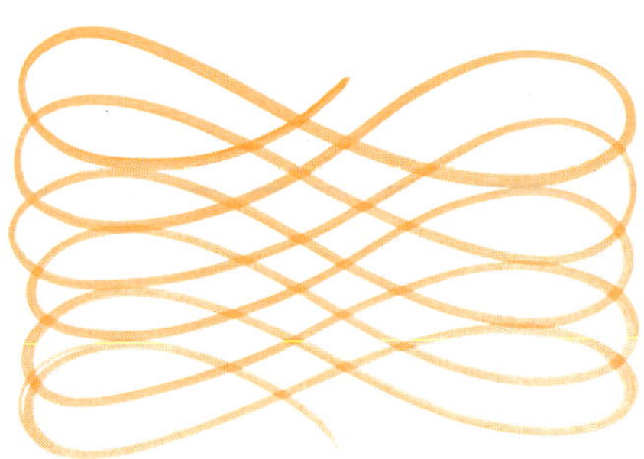

This is a fun exercise, and is best done to music. Listen to, or hum, a waltz — how about the "Blue Danube." Concentrate more on the music than the stroke. Trying to be too analytical about the stroke gets in the way of the flow of it. You might start off a little haphazardly. Don't worry. Just keep going. It will soon fall into the rhythm of the music and become uniform. Once you are comfortable with the mechanics of the stroke, start to concentrate on the execution. Strive for consistency in repetition - have each loop overlap the previous one in the same location. Be sure to hold the brush perpendicular and see that the hairs always follow the handle.

Thin your paint to a non-fat milk or an almost ink-like consistency. Thoroughly load the brush and try to paint as long a spiral as possible with one loading.

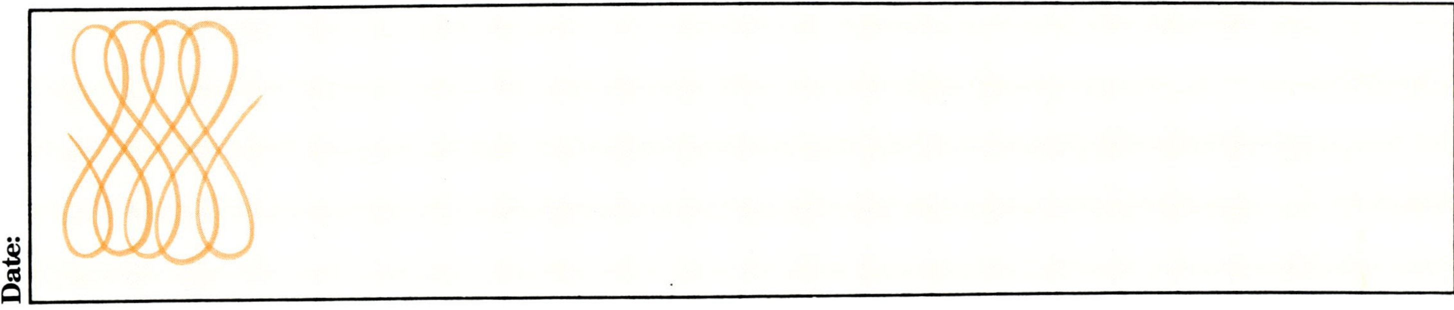

There now, wasn't that fun! Don't worry if you have lots of uneven loops. You'll soon master the rhythm and flow of this one and feel like a real pro.

WHOOPS! Let's analyze a few possible problem areas before you turn to the Magic Paper.

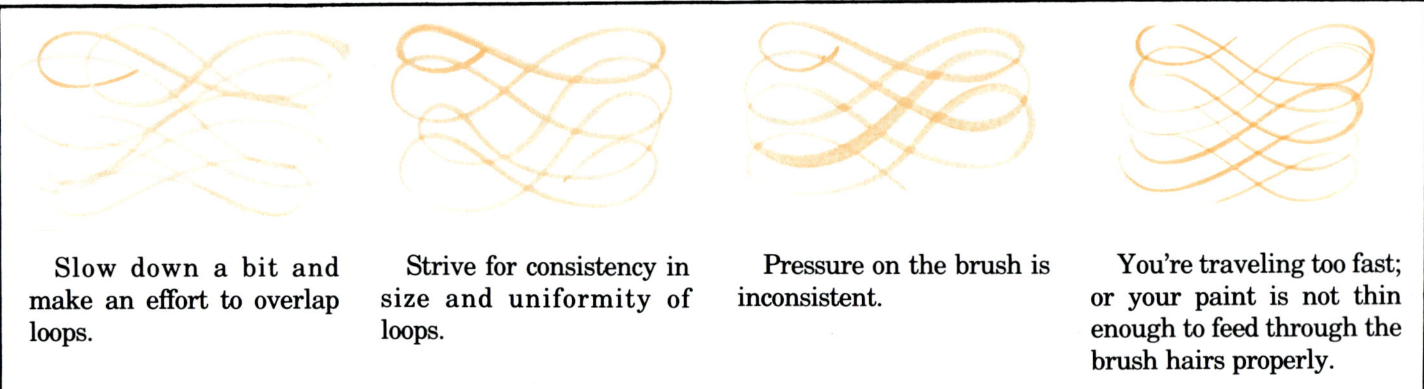

Slow down a bit and make an effort to overlap loops.

Strive for consistency in size and uniformity of loops.

Pressure on the brush is inconsistent.

You're traveling too fast; or your paint is not thin enough to feed through the brush hairs properly.

Alright! On to the Magic Paper. Imagine you're figure skating. Sing the "Skaters Waltz" and have a grand time. Fall in love with that liner and all the marvelous things you're going to be able to make it do. Later, return to this page and "show your stuff!"

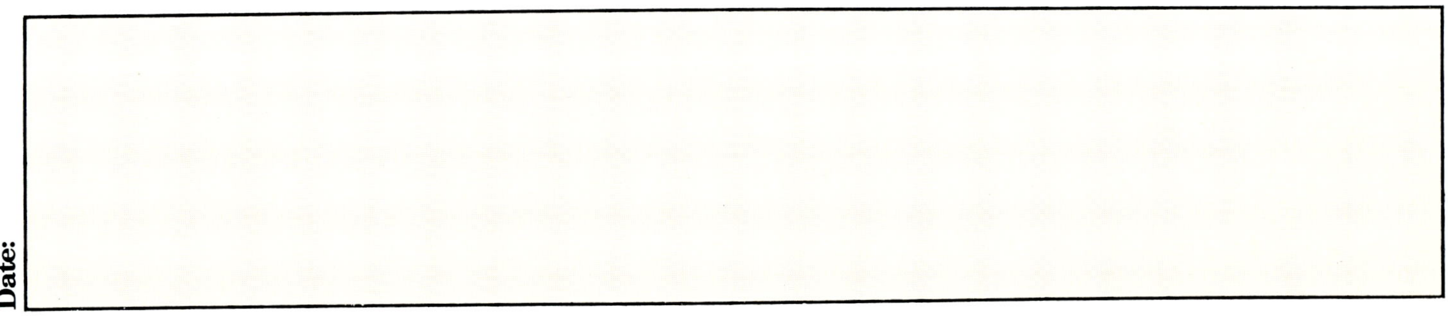

Always warm up with exercises, such as the 3 preceding ones, before painting liner work. You'll be more flowing, loose, and confident.

"S" STROKE

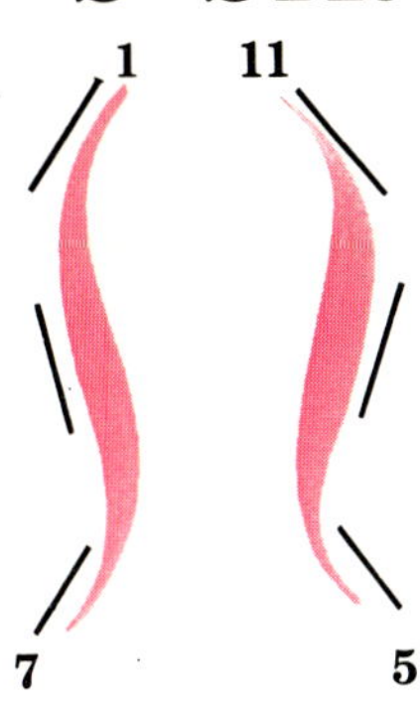

Before working on this stroke, warm up with some exercises (from 3 previous pages) on the Magic Paper. As with the flat brush "S" (covered on page 11), the liner "S" stroke is not a curvy "S" but rather a graceful Hogarth curve. It has 3 directional changes, shown by the lines on the example at left. The liner "S" should show a contrast in thick and thin pressure. Start on the tip of the brush at 1 o'clock; begin adding gradual pressure as you pull towards 7 o'clock. Continue adding more pressure as you change direction and head toward 5 o'clock. Greatest pressure is in the mid section. Gradually release pressure and change direction back to 7 o'clock. Slow down, stop and lift off. To paint an "S" facing the other way, begin at 11 o'clock, pull towards 5 o'clock, reverse to 7 o'clock and then back to 5 o'clock.

Now, you try it. Thin paint slightly. Remember to load brush thoroughly. Record today's date.

Date:

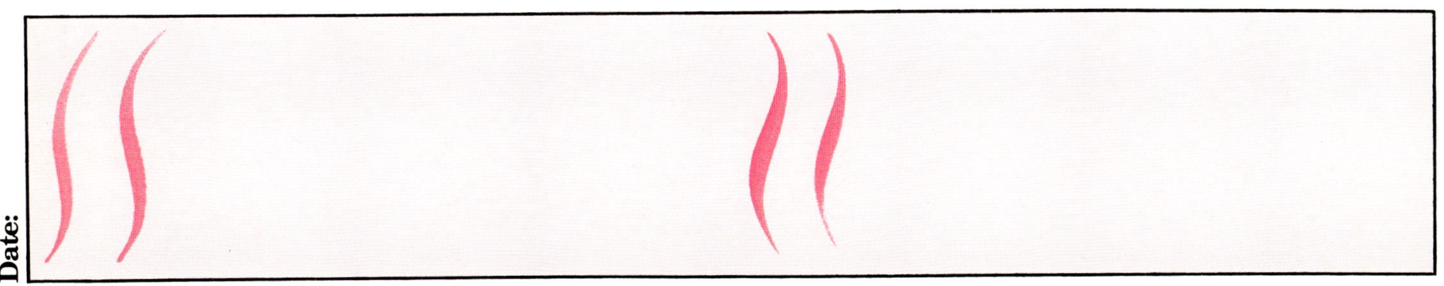

Practice both directions. Later, also practice sideways and upside down. You'll find one direction you prefer. Nevertheless, do try to master the other directions.

WHOOPS! How did you do? Did you encounter any of the usual problems below?

Too "S-ie." Straighten those curves out a bit for a more graceful flow.

You're really hooked on this one. Remember, beginning and ending should be on the same angle.

This is like what happens when you pick up a cat; everything slides to the bottom. Work on more even distribution of weight.

Angles may appear at top or bottom and result from **sudden** directional and pressure changes. **Slide** into those changes.

I know. You were having such fun, it was hard to know when to stop. Remember, however, only **three** directional changes.

Out of balance. Try to make top and bottom about the same length.

Be sure to mark your problem areas so you can focus on correcting them. Then give the Magic Paper a good "S" workout. When you return here to paint a follow up, have some fun. Paint a couple of borders.

Date:

Lefties - Turn the book upside down and work from the right.

CRESCENT STROKE

LINER AND ROUND BRUSH

This stroke, by itself, can be used to make flowers, or it may embellish the crescents made with the flat brush. Like the "S," the stroke begins on the tip of the brush. Be sure the brush is held perpendicular to the painting surface. Think of a circle as you make the stroke. Pull slightly; then gradually apply pressure, curving around; and gradually release pressure. The stroke progresses from thin to thick to thin again. Emphasise the thick and thin. Contrast makes these strokes interesting.

Thin paint slightly, and load brush thoroughly. Do you remember always to balance on your little finger? And does the little finger move with the rest of your arm and shoulder? If it gets stuck, then you'll have to **push** the brush with your thumb and fingers and that's a No No!

WHOOPS! Before checking the problem areas below, study your strokes and see if you can analyze any problems on your own. Begin now to develop a critical eye.

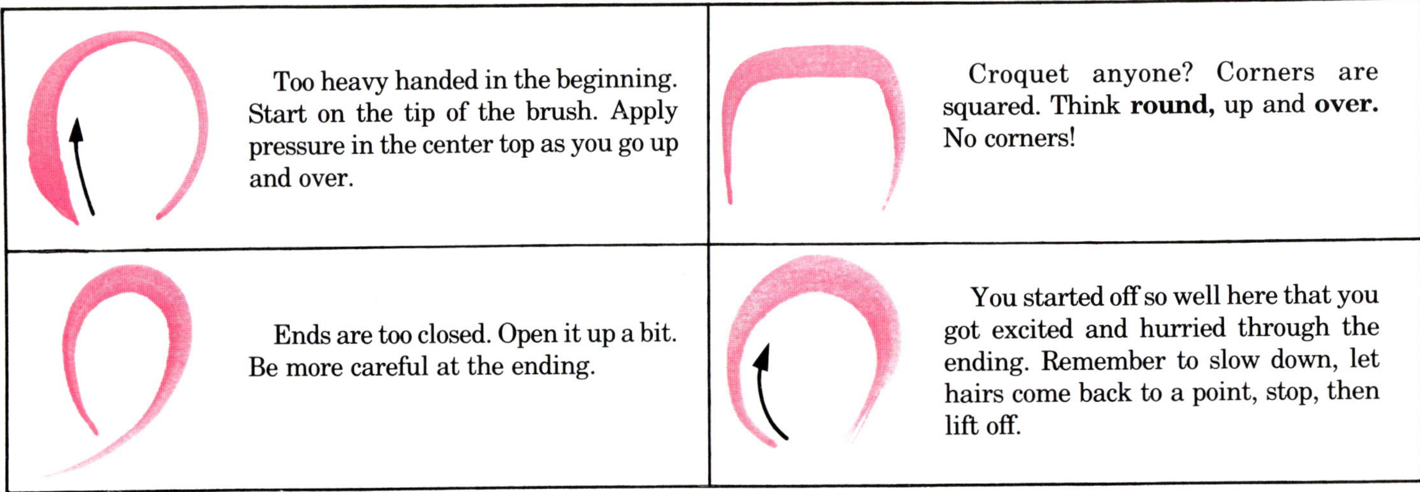

Too heavy handed in the beginning. Start on the tip of the brush. Apply pressure in the center top as you go up and over.

Croquet anyone? Corners are squared. Think **round,** up and **over.** No corners!

Ends are too closed. Open it up a bit. Be more careful at the ending.

You started off so well here that you got excited and hurried through the ending. Remember to slow down, let hairs come back to a point, stop, then lift off.

There now. With an understanding of where the weak spots are, go directly to the Magic Paper. With your cooperation, it will help you iron out the problems.

Date:

Compare your earlier strokes with these made after considerable practice. Do you see improvement?

SCROLL

LINER AND ROUND BRUSH

If you couldn't resist making too curvy "S" strokes, you'll have a great time with the scroll stroke. Like the "S," it starts thin, grows thick, and returns to thin again. Unlike the "S," it can twist and cavort in all kinds of directions. Make the stroke exciting by emphasizing the thicks and thins. Be sure to use your whole arm. A temptation to push the stroke around with thumb and fingers results in unappealing strokes. Review the warm-up exercises. You may find leaning into the curve (coil) helpful on this one. The fluid motion you learned on the double loops will also be helpful. This is a beautiful, flowing stroke, best done with the liner, although the round brush will paint a thicker scroll.

Paint should be thinned to a light cream consistency.

Lefties, turn the book upside down and work from this side.

Date:

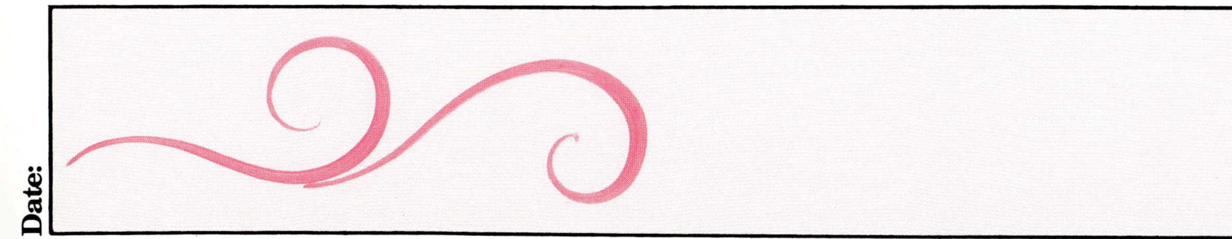

There was hardly enough room above to paint many examples, but you should be able to analyze your strengths and weaknesses.

WHOOPS!

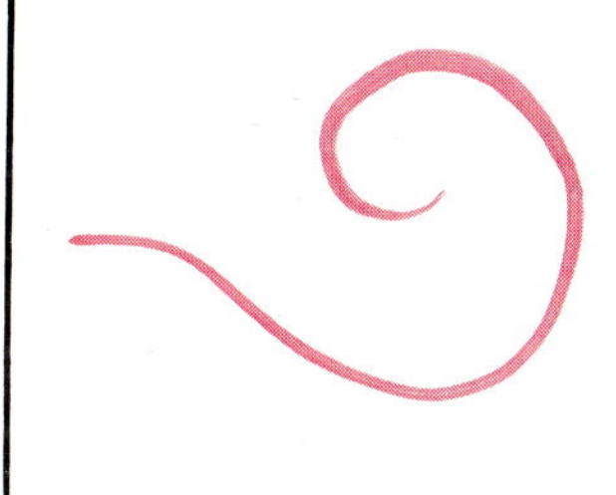

Ah hah! You used your fingers after all. Even when I cautioned you not to! Finger movements cause jerky interruptions in the graceful flow that's possible from shoulder/whole arm produced strokes. To the Magic Paper with you. Practice, practice.

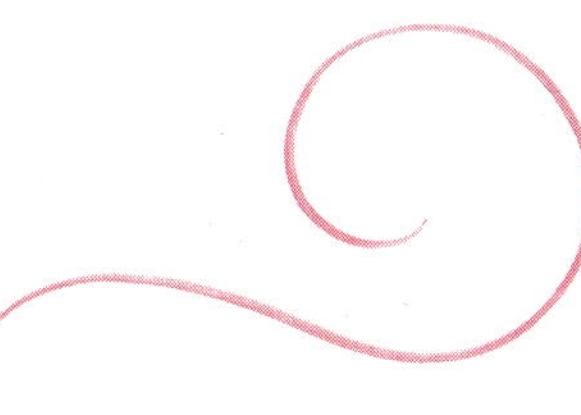

Bor-i-ng! No variation in line width. Remember, variety is the spice of life. Thick and thin contrast is certainly what gives these strokes life.

After practicing on the Magic Paper on page 9, record your progress below by painting two different scroll borders. Note the positions of the dots, showing starting positions.

Lefties, turn the book upside down again.

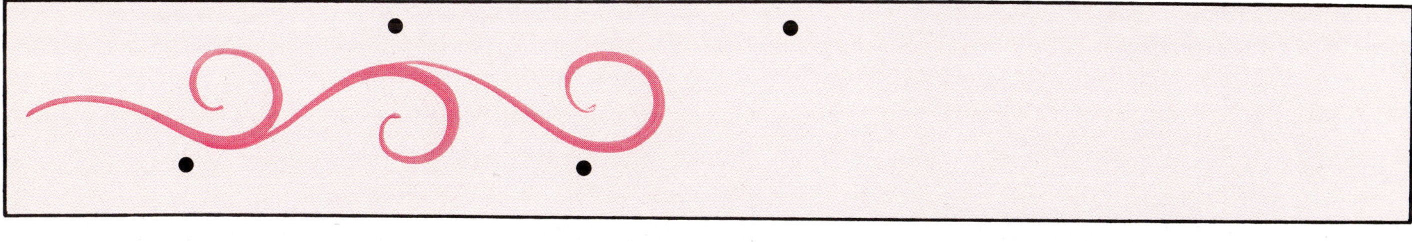

Date:

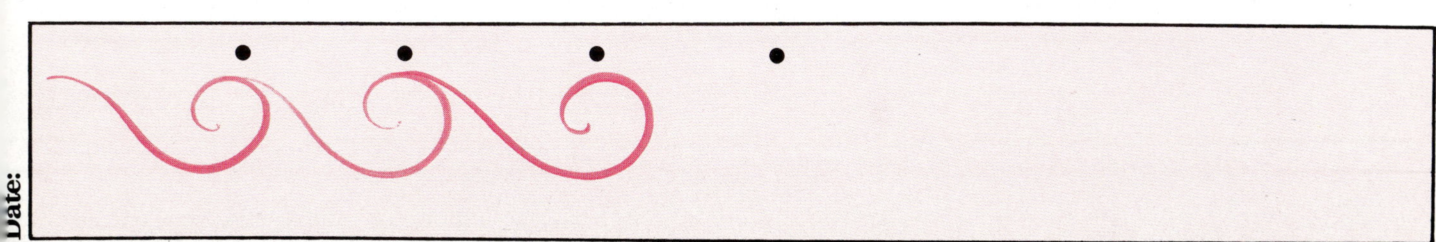

When you're confident with the scroll stroke and these two border variations, add other strokes for embellishments. See back cover.

COMMA STROKE

LINER AND ROUND BRUSH

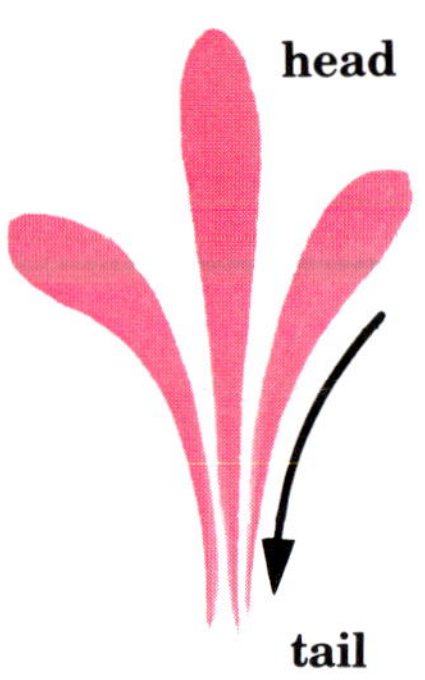

This is a stroke you'll have a lot of fun with. It makes nice borders, marvelous flowers, even moustaches and hairdos. Make it with thick paint for a richly textured stroke. Or, thin the paint slightly for a somewhat flatter stroke. Load extra paint on the tip of the brush to create a nice, rounded "head" on the stroke. Press the loaded brush down on the painting surface, causing hairs to flare out a little; pause; then begin pulling and releasing pressure on the brush. Slow down as you near the tip of the "tail" of the stroke, letting hairs return to the point. Stop, then lift off. Try the strokes curving to left, to right, straight up, sideways, and upside down.

Practice comma strokes large and small, in all directions. Remember to record the date.

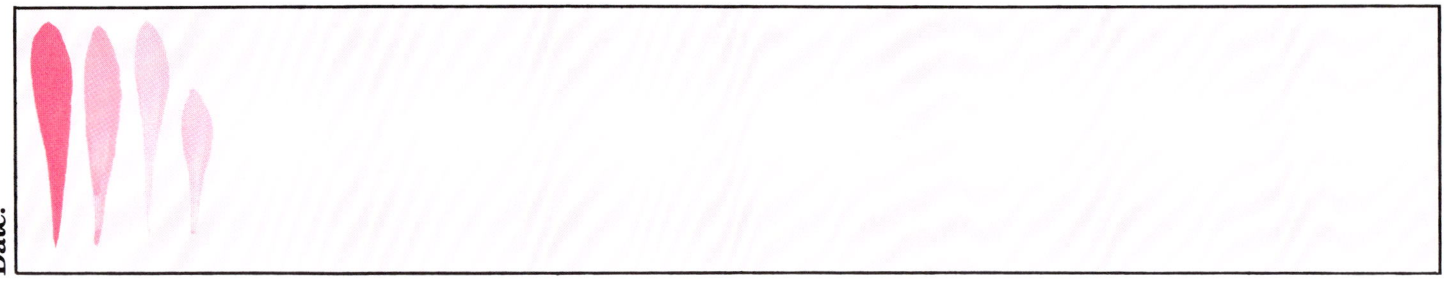

Date:

WHOOPS!

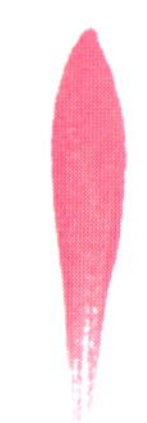

Still in a hurry, eh? When will you learn to slow down! Let the brush hairs return to their natural configuration, stop, **then** lift off. You can also get fuzzy "tails" from bad brushes - ones which no longer come to a fine point. Have you let paint dry and harden in your brush up in the metal ferrule? See page 22.

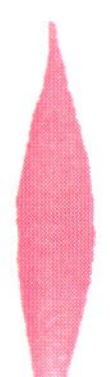

A point on the head of the stroke can result from: 1) having failed to load extra paint on the tip, particularly on the fine pointed liners; 2) pulling the stroke as soon as the brush was set down without pausing to permit hairs to spread to form the rounded head.

Did you forget how to release pressure gradually? Too sudden a release of pressure causes abrupt changes as shown here. Let your little finger act as a lever to help raise your whole hand (and thus the brush), gradually decreasing pressure.

Mark your trouble spots in the practice strip above, then turn to page 9 to practice. Make a follow-up sample here when you're nearly great.

Date:

Now that you are becoming so well versed in strokes, you aren't forgetting to practice all your earlier strokes and warm up exercises, are you?

TEARDROP STROKE

LINER AND ROUND BRUSH

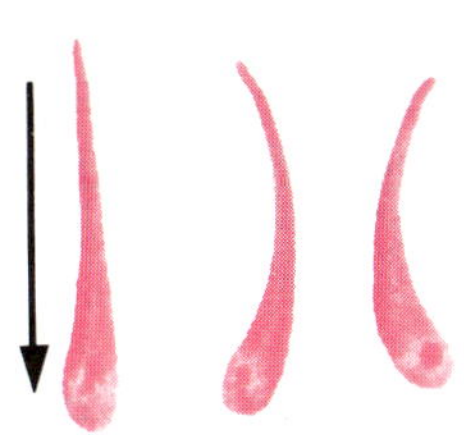

This stroke, at first glance, looks very much like a comma stroke. But, as you will observe when you paint samples of each, the teardrop has a little collection of paint which is deposited in the head, whereas the paint flows smoothly through the head of the comma stroke. The teardrop is begun on the tip of the brush at the tip of the "tail" of the stroke. Pull and gradually press to form "head." Lift straight off. Keep brush perpendicular to your painting surface.

Hint: Load more paint in the middle of the brush. Stroke excess paint out of the tip onto the palette. This is a very spontaneous stroke once you've mastered it.

Practice these straight as illustrated, to start. Later, curve them and do them sideways and upside down. Thin paint slightly, (light cream consistency).

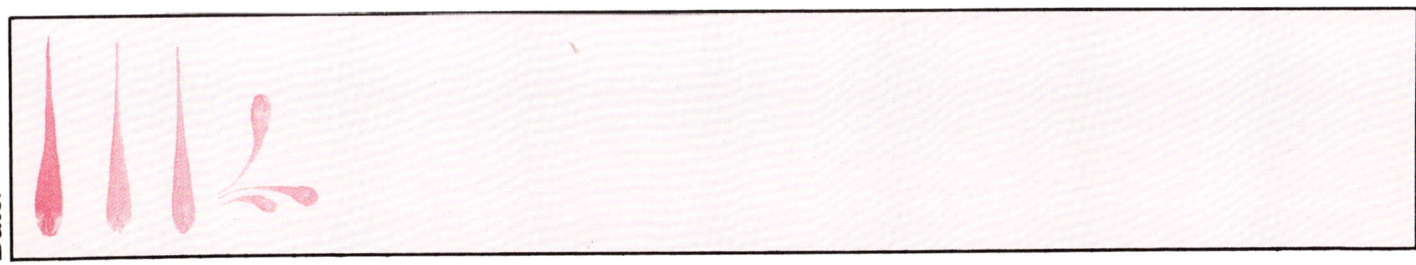

Date:

WHOOPS! There are several things that can go awry when you first start making this stroke. How many problems can you locate in your first practice sample.

A fat beginning — a common problem. It's hard to set the brush gently down and pull a skinny line. Remedy: imagine you're an airplane coming in for a landing. Begin the stroke in the air, slightly. As you swoop down onto the paper, you should already be pulling the stroke. Keep going and then press to a head. In the beginning, it will be hard to judge where strokes will "land." That comes with practice.

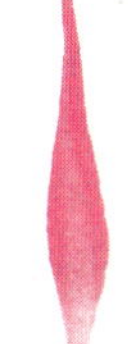

A good beginning but you pulled the tip of the brush through the head. Remember: Slow down, stop, then lift off — don't continue pulling.

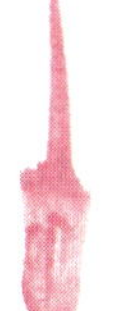

Abrupt shoulders on the stroke result from pushing back toward the tail when trying to lift off. Notice where the tip of the brush is when you stop. Be sure it doesn't either slide back or pull forward as you lift off.

Not quite a teardrop. There's no gradual change in pressure. The stroke went from skinny to fat. (This does make nice flower stamens, however.)

This is a great stroke to practice on Magic Paper. Remember to be an airplane and glide in for a landing. Paint a follow-up sample below once you're satisfied with your progress.

Date:

Well now, you've just worked your way through eleven strokes and three warm up exercises. You'll soon be well on your way to becoming a bonafide decorative painter. To learn about more strokes and flower and leaf combinations, ask at your favorite painting store for **Jackie's Freehanding Seminar, Book 1.** For a collection of over 200 brush stroke border designs, see **Freehanding With Jackie**. And for beginning stroke design projects, see **The Beginner's Guide to Freehand Decorative Painting.**

CARE AND HANDLING OF BRUSHES

Your brushes represent a good investment. Treat them with care and respect, and they will work well for you and last longer.

FOR ACRYLICS

1. Clean your brushes often and thoroughly. A quick swish through the water is **not** enough. Use Ivory soap or Loew-Cornell's Brush Cleaner for Acrylic Paints and with your fingers gently work the soap into the hairs. Rinse. Continue soaping and rinsing until every trace of color is gone! Paint allowed to harden in your brush, even in minute amounts, eventually creates a hard "knot" up near the metal ferrule. This "knot" causes the hairs to separate and thereby reduces the effectiveness of the brush. A brush thus damaged can sometimes be partially restored by cleaning with a solvent such as nail polish remover, alcohol, or some of the commercially prepared acrylic paint removers/brush cleaners. This is a harsh measure so should be resorted to only when absolutely necessary. Keep solvent away from the handle as it will penetrate the lacquer and create a very sticky situation.

2. After thoroughly cleaning the brush, put more Ivory soap into it and reshape the hairs. Shape round and liner brush hairs to a fine point. Shape flat brushes to a smooth chisel edge. Dry. The hairs should be quite stiff. This helps them to retain their crisp shapes, and minimizes damage in storage. Thoroughly rinse all soap from the brush before using again.

FOR OILS

1. Upon completion of painting, rinse brushes thoroughly in paint thinner or turpentine. (Keep this solvent capped during painting to prevent your breathing harmful fumes.)

2. Dip the hairs in lard oil (available through many art and craft stores) or use vegetable oil in a pinch. Work the oil up into the hairs causing trapped pigment to disperse. Wipe clean and repeat until all trace of color has disappeared. After thoroughly cleaning the brush, put more lard oil into it and reshape the hair to a point or chisel edge depending upon the brush.

Note: Oil painting brushes may also be cleaned and shaped with soap and water following a good rinsing in thinner. See steps 1 and 2 for acrylics. Before using the brush in oil paint again, rinse soap out in thinner. Lard oil may be simply wiped out gently on a paper towel.

FOR WATERCOLORS

1. Generally, a good strong swishing in water is sufficient. If the hairs are stained by a strong pigment however, wash gently with Ivory soap until color disappears. (Note: White nylon may discolor permanently, but that will not affect the brush.)

2. Rinse brushes thoroughly, re-shape flats to a sharp chisel edge, rounds and liners to a point.

STORAGE OF BRUSHES

Store the brushes so the hairs will not be bent or crushed. Some possibilities include: a) weave them into a woven placemat which can be rolled up and tied with ribbon for storage or travel; b) fasten them to cardboard with elastic or rubber bands; c) stand them on their handle ends in a glass or jar; d) store them in commercially available cases specially designed to separate the brushes and keep them from shifting.

If you are using red sable brushes for oils or watercolors, and if you live in an area where moths are a problem, store a few mothballs or moth crystals with your brushes to prevent damage.

NEED HELP FINDING SPARE TIME TO PRACTICE?

1. Whenever you're stuck on the phone, dip your brush in water and practice.

2. When you must drive the carpool and wait and wait - carry along a cup of water, brush and your book with the Magic Paper. Practice.

3. Insomnia! Keep a cup of water, brush and book by your bedside.

4. Eating alone and bored? Set an extra place - just a cup of water and brush will do. Turn to page 9 and PRACTICE.

5. Watching the soaps, sitcoms, superbowl? Or perhaps **you're not** watching the superbowl. At any rate, during — or in spite of — T.V., Practice! Magic Paper makes it painless.

Learn to paint strokes in all possible directions. Some ways will be easier for you than others. No matter. Learn them all. Some day, you may become a wall decorator of international fame. And it really wouldn't do, would it, for you to be on the scaffolding fifty-two feet in the air standing on your head doing a particular stroke because you never learned to paint that one upside down! Practice strokes very large and very small. Push your brush to extremes.

JACKIE SHAW'S DECORATIVE DESIGN STUDIO PUBLICATIONS

Introduce you to the many facets of decorative painting

Now that you have begun to paint here are some other types of decorative painting techniques you may wish to explore — and the Decorative Design Studio books by many talented authors to guide you on your way.

BASIC TECHNIQUES

#39 Jackie's Brush Stroke Workbook $ 6.95
(Part I of Fun-damentals of Freehanding Series)

#40 Beginner's Guide to Freehand Decorative Painting $ 8.95
(Part 2 of Fun-damentals of Freehanding Series)

#4 Tole Techniques and Decorative Arts, Vol. 4 $ 3.95

#5 There's A Rainbow In My Paintbox $ 5.95

#6 Pigments of Your Imagination, Vol. 1 $ 5.95

#7 Pigments of Your Imagination, Vol. 2 $ 5.95

***FUN*-DAMENTALS OF FREEHANDING**

PART 1

#39 Jackie's Brush Stroke Workbook $ 6.95

PART 2

#40 Beginners Guide to Freehand Decorative Painting $ 8.95

PART 3

#9 Freehanding With Jackie $ 6.95

PART 4

#24 Jackie's Freehanding Seminar, Book 1 $ 8.95

DECORATIVE FOLK ART

#10 Rock 'N Tole $ 8.50

#19 Freehanding On The Wind $ 4.95

#12 Jackie's Toybox $ 8.95

#15 Painting In The Pantry With Jackie $ 5.50

#94 Jackie's Painting Menagerie $ 2.99

#27 Jackie's Golden Goose $ 6.95

#23 Country Harvest $ 6.50

#32 Forget The Dust — Let's Paint! $ 6.95

PAINTING ON WOOD CUTOUTS

#25 Sweet, Soft And Country $ 6.50

#29 Country Lovin' $ 7.50

#26 Ardi's Country Painting, Book 1 $ 6.95

#30 Ardi's Country Painting, Book 2 $ 6.95

#36 Ardi's Country Painting, Book 3 $ 6.95

#41 Ardi's Country Painting, Book 4 $ 6.95

#47 Ardi's Country Painting, Book 5 $ 6.95

#43 Melodies from the Heart $ 5.95

#37 Homespun Memories, Vol. 1 $ 6.95

#45 Homespun Memories, Vol. 2 $ 6.95

#46 Something to Quack About, Vol. 1 $ 6.95

STENCILING

#93 Stencil Designs from the Old Stone Mill $ 4.95

#28 Classic Stenciling with Bronze Powders $ 5.95

SILK PAINTING

#33 Introduction To Silk Painting $ 5.95

REALISTIC PAINTING

#38 You Can Paint Anything in Oils or Acrylics $ 7.95

EUROPEAN FOLK ART

#34 Hindeloopen — A Traditional Dutch Folk Painting $10.95

#31 A Ukrainian Heritage — Petrikivka Painting $ 8.95

ORIENTAL PAINTING

#11 The Scholarly Bamboo — Chinese Brush Strokes $ 9.50

#17 Tole With An Oriental Touch $ 6.75

#18 Chinoiserie For The Decorative Artist $ 5.50

FABRIC PAINTING

#16 Fabric Painting In Tole, Vol. 1 $ 7.95

#20 Fabric Painting In Tole, Vol. 2 $ 6.95

#42 Don't Sweat It, Paint It $ 6.95

#44 Paint Around Your Collar $ 5.95

CHRISTMAS

#22 Christmas At The Old Stone Mill $ 6.95

PAINTING AND TIN PUNCH

#92 Tole Painting On Country Punched Tin $ 6.95

LAMPSHADE MAKING AND DECORATING

#13 Shades of Yesteryear $ 7.50

PAINTING AND SOFT SCULPTURE

#14 Unicorns In Soft Sculpture $ 3.50

WATERCOLOR STYLE PAINTING

#35 The Acrylic Watercolor Book $ 8.95

BRUSH KITS

#90 Basic Brush Kit $10.15

#91 Decorative Folk Art Kit $37.95

Books are available at your favorite craft supply store, or you may order direct from the publisher. When ordering direct, include **$1.50** for postage and handling for up to 3 books, plus 15¢ for each additional book. A descriptive brochure is available for $1.00. Write Jackie Shaw's Decorative Design Studio, Inc., The Old Stone Mill, Rt. 3, Box 155, Smithsburg, MD 21783. *Prices subject to change.*

SOME SIMPLE DESIGNS AND BORDERS TO PRACTICE

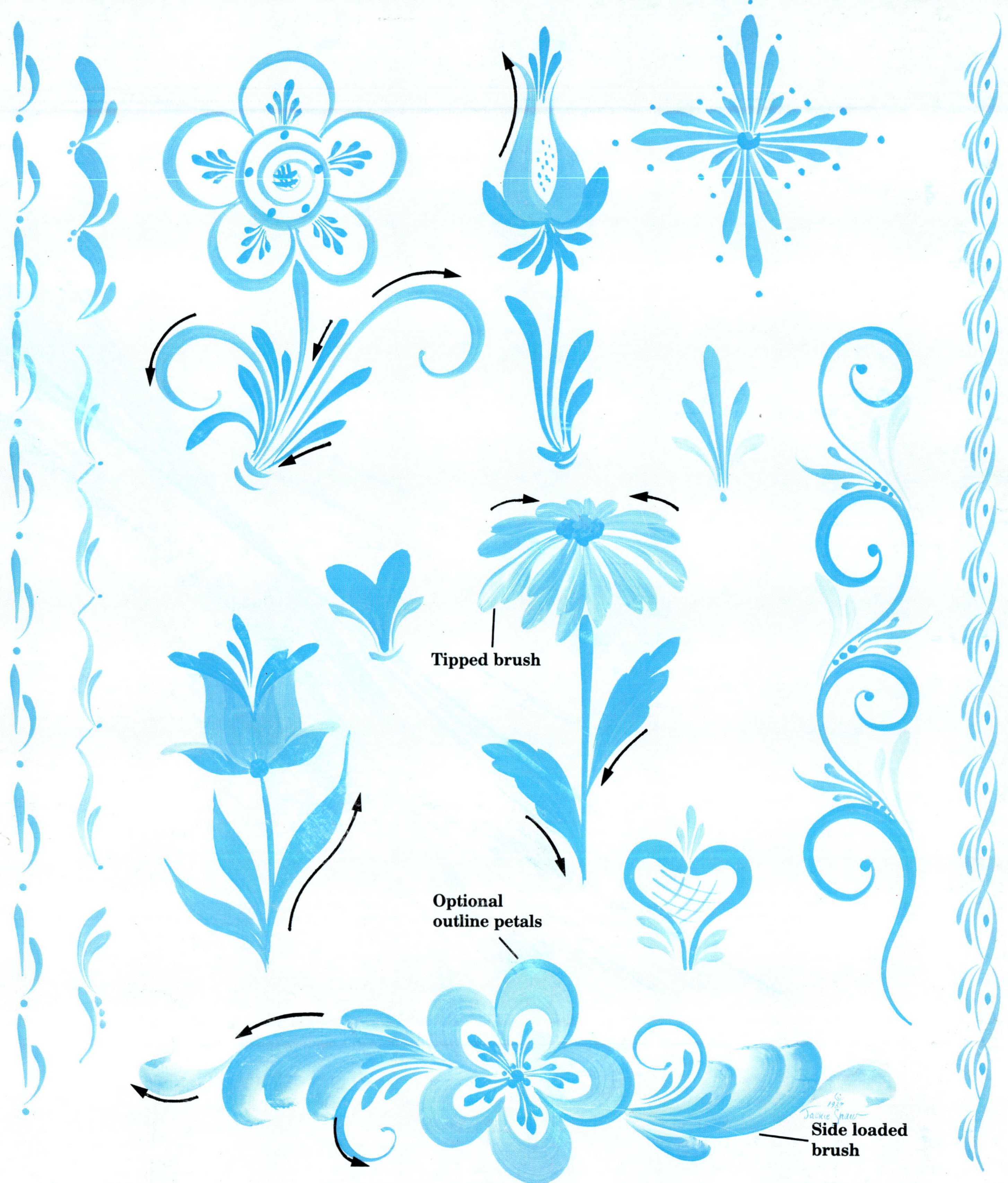

To keep strokes in borders fairly even in size, always glance at your first couple of strokes before adding a new stroke. Do not refer to the most recent stroke made. Strokes trend to grow as you paint.

> Hint: Work with a friend. Trade workbooks for critiquing. It's often easier to spot someone else's mistakes and help them to correct technique than it is to correct your own.

ISBN 0-941284-39-5